LITTLE CHICKS NEST EGG

By Alison Delaney.
Illustrated by Stuart Perry.

Published by: Little Bird Products.

ISBN: 978-0-9934907-2-9

Designed by Stuart Perry.

I send a special thanks to our Partners, who have enabled us to empower thousands of children through their sponsorship.

Little chick knows if he has a scheme
He'll be clear on how big he can dream
Now he'll explore how he can achieve
By living in the now and knowing what to leave.

Little chick knows exactly what he ate
And always saved seeds for a later date
It meant he could help our miserable mouse
When he found him hungry outside his house.

Miserable mouse didnt plan for tomorrow
When he ran out of seeds he had to borrow
And now it was time for him to pay back
All the seeds he had borrowed to fill his own sack
He paid chick back with some extra seeds
But had nothing left for his very own needs.

Have one for today and two for tomorrow
That way you know, you won't need to borrow.

Little chick knew there were lessons to learn
So decided to take mouse through the thick forest fern
There in the shadows was a little oak tree
They could hear lots of scratching but what could it be?

Squirrel popped out with hands full of nuts
Then scampered away into a wooden hut
Chick said to mouse, that's squirrels store
Let's see if we can find out some more.

Squirrel, Squirrel, would you come and share
Why you're taking those nuts from over here to there?
Squirrel smiled and told chick and mouse
I'm saving my acorns to buy a big house
I have 1 today and 2 for tomorrow
That way you see, I won't need to borrow.

Mouse asked squirrel what will you pay
To buy your big house and on what day?
30 acorns is what I'll pay
Can work out on what day?

EXERCISE:
If squirrel collects 3 acorns every day, each day
eats 1 and saves 2, how many days will it take to
save 30 acorns?

Mouse was learning the need to save
As he had his heart set on buying a cave
A place where all of his family could live
This is a gift he would love to give
So 1 for today and 2 for tomorrow
That means he won't need to borrow

Little chick knew of mouses big idea
And wanted mouse to be really clear
There's more than one way to have a home
Let's go and see badger at the woodland dome

Over the mossy bramble floor
They soon arrived at a big oak door
Mouse gave the door a great big knock
And stood back as it started to unlock

With a creak and a squeak the door opened up
And badger appeared holding a biscuit and cup
Hi mouse, hi chick, please come on through
What is it that I can do for you?

Chick asked badger to share her story
Of her home in all it's glory
I first built a home that was just for me
Then I worked hard and built another three
6 months later, I'd built another 7
And by the end of the year, another eleven.

$$1 + 3 + 7 + 11 =$$

Now lots of badgers live in the dome
It's a safe and warm place they can call home
Each month I get 3 berries per let
But I haven't worked out the yearly total yet
I live in my own home for free
Can you tell me what my yearly total will be?

Remember the lesson chick said to mouse
If you want that cave for your future house
When you find seeds, put some aside
Then you can take life in your stride
It's easy to do if you work hard and think
Said little chick, and gave mouse a wink.

Have 1 for today and 2 for tomorrow
That means you won't need to borrow.

I'M SAVING FOR...

_____

_____

_____

_____

_____